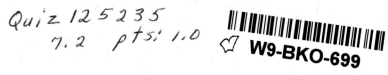

Quiz 125235
7.2 pts: 1.0

W9-BKO-699

THE NHL: HISTORY AND HEROES

CHICAGO BLACKHAWKS

Published by Creative Education
P.O. Box 227, Mankato, Minnesota 56002
Creative Education is an imprint of The Creative Company.

DESIGN AND PRODUCTION BY **ZENO DESIGN**

Printed in the United States of America

PHOTOGRAPHS BY Corbis (Bettmann), Getty Images (Bruce Bennett Studios, Tony Biegun, Jonathan Daniel, DEA/S.AMANTINI, Henry DiRocco, Focus on Sport, William Huber, Wallace Kirkland//Time Life Pictures, Robert Laberge/ALLSPORT, Phillip MacCallum, Francis Miller//Time Life Pictures, Frank Scherschel/Time & Life Pictures, Rick Stewart), Hockey Hall of Fame (Imperial Oil-Turofsky)

LIBRARY OF CONGRESS CATALOGING-IN-PUBLICATION DATA

Skog, Jason.
The story of the Chicago Blackhawks / by Jason Skog.
p. cm. — (The NHL: history and heroes)
Includes index
ISBN 978-1-58341-615-0
1. Chicago Blackhawks (Hockey team)—History—Juvenile Literature. I. Title. II. Series.

GV848.C48S54 2008
796.962'640977311—dc22   2007014998

First Edition

9 8 7 6 5 4 3 2 1

COVER: Wing Patrick Kane

JASON SKOG

THE NHL: HISTORY AND HEROES

CHICAGO

BLACKHAWKS

TRAILING 1–0 WITH A MAN IN THE PENALTY BOX, THE CHICAGO BLACKHAWKS WERE IN A TIGHT SPOT. THE RIVAL DETROIT RED WINGS HAD THE MOMENTUM—AND A LOUD OLYMPIA STADIUM CROWD—ON THEIR SIDE IN GAME 6 OF THE 1961 STANLEY CUP FINALS. BUT THE TIDE TURNED WHEN BLACKHAWKS DEFENSEMAN REG FLEMING BROKE UP THE RED WINGS' POWER PLAY AND STOLE THE PUCK. FLEMING RACED TO THE DETROIT END AND SLAPPED A SHOT PAST RED WINGS GOALIE HANK BASSEN. THE GOAL FIRED UP THE BLACKHAWKS, WHO POURED IN FOUR MORE

BLACKHAWKS

TO WIN THE GAME 5–1 AND TAKE THE BEST-OF-SEVEN STANLEY CUP SERIES FOUR GAMES TO TWO. WHEN THE GAME ENDED, CHICAGO'S PLAYERS CIRCLED THE CUP IN CELEBRATION BUT DECLINED TO PARADE IT AROUND BEFORE THE SILENCED CROWD. THEY SAVED THEIR CELEBRATION FOR THE LOCKER ROOM, WHERE PLAYERS ERUPTED IN ROARS OF EMOTION. THEY WERE TAKING THE STANLEY CUP BACK HOME TO CHICAGO FOR THE FIRST TIME IN 23 YEARS.

THE BLACKHAWKS BEGIN

FOUNDED ON THE SOUTHERN TIP OF Lake Michigan, Chicago, Illinois, is famous for its strong breezes, deep-dish pizza, and towering skyline. As the third-largest city in the United States, it is also the business, financial, and cultural center of the Midwest. Chicago is nicknamed the "Windy City" and is sometimes called the "City of Broad Shoulders" due to the resilient and hardworking nature of its citizens.

Chicago is also known for its passion for sports. Home to more than 15 professional sports franchises, Chicago was named the best sports city in America by *The Sporting News* in 2006. Among the city's oldest and most adored teams is the National Hockey League's (NHL) Chicago Blackhawks. Founded in

Founded in the 1830s, Chicago has since grown into a vast metropolis, home to world-famous skyscrapers, museums, and many sports franchises.

1926, the Blackhawks were an instant hit in the Illinois metropolis. And it all began with a telephone call.

In the mid-1920s, brothers Frank and Lester Patrick owned the struggling Western Hockey League (WHL). Faced with the prospect of selling off their teams, the brothers placed a call to Major Frederic McLaughlin to see if he was interested in buying one of the WHL clubs. McLaughlin, a Chicago native who had prospered in the coffee business, put together an investment group of his wealthy friends and bought the Rosebuds of Portland, Oregon, for $200,000. McLaughlin renamed his squad the Blackhawks and found it a home in the Chicago Coliseum.

In their debut on November 17, 1926, the fledgling Blackhawks defeated the Toronto St. Patricks 4–1 before a sold-out Coliseum crowd. The team came to Chicago with a fair amount of talent, including a trio of speedy forwards:

Stan Mikita CENTER

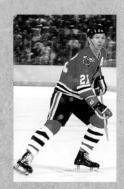

During his 22 seasons with the Blackhawks, Stan Mikita scored 541 goals, putting him second on the NHL's all-time scoring list when he left the game. He played in a team-record 1,394 NHL games over that stretch. But his biggest contribution to hockey may have been the slight curve he added to the blade of his stick. Mikita discovered that the curve could make the puck swoop and dip, and the modification soon became a league standard. Mikita was the first Czechoslovakian-born player in the NHL, opening the door for the dozens of his countrymen who have since played in the league.

BLACKHAWKS SEASONS: 1958–80
HEIGHT: 5-9 (175 cm)
WEIGHT: 169 (77 kg)

- 4-time Art Ross Trophy winner (as NHL points leader)
- 2-time Hart Trophy winner (as league MVP)
- 926 career assists
- Hockey Hall of Fame inductee (1983)

The Blackhawks (shown here wearing the back-striped sweaters) started out slowly, posting the NHL's worst records in 1927–28 and 1928–29.

Charles "Rabbit" McVeigh, Dick Irvin, and Mickey MacKay. But the most effective player that first season was wing Cecil "Babe" Dye, who was brought in from Toronto. Boasting one of the most feared slap shots in all of hockey, Dye finished second in the NHL in goals scored during his first season with the Blackhawks. The team ended its opening campaign in third place in its division. Disappointed with the finish, McLaughlin promptly fired coach Pete Muldoon. It was just the first in a string of coaching changes McLaughlin would make.

"The coach is an important man on a hockey club. But never for a minute forget that no matter who the coach is, he can't put the puck in the net from the bench."

CHICAGO COACH DICK IRVIN

Chicago's second season was also disappointing, as it finished last among the American Division's five teams and missed the playoffs. But there was a glimmer of hope in new goaltender Charlie Gardiner. Gardiner was young but was clearly a star on the rise, showing an uncanny ability to predict opponents' moves as they approached with the puck.

In 1928–29, the Blackhawks won just 7 games all season and played their last 16 games on the road after McLaughlin let his lease on the Chicago Coliseum expire. But the team was preparing to move into the new Chicago Stadium the next year, and it was prepared to start winning.

The Muldoon Curse

ACCORDING TO LEGEND, THE BLACKHAWKS skated under a curse for the first 40 years of their existence. The Blackhawks played their first season in 1926–27. The team had a respected coach in Pete Muldoon and some talented players, including wing Babe Dye. Dye was a mediocre skater but was said to have the hardest slap shot in hockey. He finished that season with the second-highest goal total in the league, and the Blackhawks finished third in the new American Division. But the performance wasn't good enough for the team's owner, Major Frederic McLaughlin, who fired Muldoon after the season's last game. As the legend goes, Muldoon was furious and warned McLaughlin that he would regret his decision. "The Hawks will never finish first!" Muldoon yelled. "I'll put a curse on this team that will hoodoo it." The team seemed to struggle from that point on. During the next year's training camp, Dye broke his leg in a scrimmage prank, and over the next 13 years, McLaughlin would make 13 coaching changes. The Blackhawks won the Stanley Cup in 1934, but they wouldn't finish first in the NHL standings until the 1966–67 season.

NEW STADIUM SPELLS SUCCESS

THE HUGE NEW BUILDING ON WEST MADISON
Street in downtown Chicago could hold almost
18,000 people, making it the largest arena in the
league. In their new home, the Blackhawks soon
became one of the NHL's elite teams.

In 1933–34, Chicago finished second to the Detroit
Red Wings in the American Division. That season,
the Blackhawks had a strong lineup—and a bunch
of nicknames—in front of Gardiner. Elwyn Nelson
"Doc" Romnes was a center known for his consistent
and clean play; wing Harold "Mush" March was one
of the few players to successfully jump from junior
hockey leagues to the NHL; and 225-pound (102 kg)
defenseman Clarence "Taffy" Abel was an intimidat-
ing presence on the ice. Gardiner, meanwhile, was
in fine form, posting 10 shutouts on the season.

Built at a cost of $9.5 million, Chicago Stadium was the largest indoor arena in the world when completed in 1929, holding 17,300 fans for hockey games.

After beating the Montreal Canadiens in the first round of the 1934 play-offs, the Hawks upset the Montreal Maroons in the semifinals. Chicago then toppled Detroit in the best-of-five Stanley Cup Finals, taking home the big silver chalice for the first time. Gardiner collected additional hardware in the form of the Vezina Trophy, awarded annually to the league's top goalie. "He would come far out of the nets and sprawl on the ice in an effort to stop a score," noted sportswriter Ron McAllister. "And even when his own team had folded up, he fought on and tried to defend his goal."

Chicago hockey fans were flying high, but just two months later, joy turned to sorrow as Gardiner collapsed and died. Without their talented netminder, the somber Blackhawks declined over the next few seasons and missed the playoffs in 1937.

To turn things back around, McLaughlin began to rebuild, signing such players as defenseman Earl Seibert. Seibert, a future Hall-of-Famer, was a hard

Bobby Hull WING

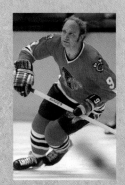

With 604 career goals in a Blackhawks sweater, Bobby Hull remains Chicago's all-time leading scorer and is considered the greatest left wing in team—and perhaps NHL—history. Early in his career, he picked up the nickname "The Golden Jet" on account of his flowing blond hair, great skating speed, and blistering slap shot. Not only was Hull a solid scorer, he was a classy player as well, winning the Lady Byng Trophy for sportsmanship after the 1964–65 season. Bobby and his son Brett are the only father-son combination to each win the Hart Trophy as league MVP.

BLACKHAWKS SEASONS: 1957–72
HEIGHT: 5-10 (178 cm)
WEIGHT: 191 (87 kg)

- 12-time All-Star
- 3-time Art Ross Trophy winner
- 2-time Hart Trophy winner
- Hockey Hall of Fame inductee (1983)

Harold "Mush" March (left) earned a special place in team history by scoring the Stanley Cup–clinching goal in Game 4 of the 1934 Finals.

checker, and when it came to fighting, few dared to challenge him. Chicago also had an up-and-coming goalie ready to replace Gardiner. Mike Karakas was a lightning-quick goaltender who had won the Calder Trophy as NHL Rookie of the Year in 1936. And in 1937, McLaughlin hired Bill Stewart—a former American League baseball umpire and NHL referee—to coach his squad.

The Blackhawks achieved a measly 14 wins in 1937–38 but managed to sneak into the playoffs. Then they embarked on one of the most extraordinary postseason runs in the history of pro sports. The Blackhawks upset the Montreal Canadiens, winning the last two games in the best-of-three series, then shocked the hockey world by following the same formula to defeat the New York Americans. Incredibly, the Hawks found themselves in the Cup Finals opposite the Toronto Maple Leafs.

With Karakas nursing a broken toe, Chicago's hopes looked slim. But the team called up minor-league goalie Alfie Moore, who led Chicago to a 3–1 victory in Game 1. The Blackhawks lost Game 2, but Karakas was back in the nets with a steel-toed skate for Game 3. In front of record-setting Chicago crowds, the Blackhawks stunned the Maple Leafs by winning the next two games to capture the Cup. "We just took the playoffs one game at a time," explained center Cully Dahlstrom. "I guess as a team we surprised quite a few people that year."

Gardiner's Glory

THE BLACKHAWKS WON THEIR FIRST Stanley Cup thanks largely to one player: goaltender Charlie Gardiner. In the 1933–34 season, the team finished second to the Detroit Red Wings in the American Division. That year, Gardiner allowed a mere 83 goals in 48 games and posted 10 shutouts. But near the end of the season, Gardiner seemed different. In spite of his strong performance between the pipes, Gardiner appeared tired and depressed. Fans speculated on the reasons for the change, but it soon became clear that Gardiner was seriously ill. It was later learned that he had a chronic tonsil infection.

Still, Gardiner continued tending the nets for the Blackhawks in the Stanley Cup Finals against the Red Wings. After losing the third game 5–2, an exhausted Gardiner told his teammates, "Look, all I want is one goal next game. Just one goal, and I'll take care of the other guys." In Game 4, Gardiner blanked Detroit, wing Mush March scored that one goal in double overtime, and the Blackhawks hoisted their first Cup. Sadly, just two months after the inspiring victory, Gardiner collapsed in his hometown of Winnipeg, Manitoba, and died of a brain hemorrhage. He was only 29 years old.

MOVING ON WITHOUT THE MAJOR

AFTER THEIR 1938 CHAMPIONSHIP, the Blackhawks slipped into a long stretch of losing hockey. Their prospects dimmed further when Major McLaughlin, the team's founder and longtime owner, died in 1944.

During the 12 seasons from 1946–47 to 1957–58, the Blackhawks made the playoffs only once. Still, there were highlights. Among them was the "Pony Line," a talented trio of fast-skating forwards—brothers Max and Doug Bentley and Bill Mosienko—that was among the most exciting of the era. While the famed line brought the Hawks scant postseason success, its members won legions of fans with their spectacular passing flair and scoring ability.

Bill Mosienko (left), a steady scorer, and Max Bentley (right), known for his dazzling offensive moves, made up two-thirds of the famed "Pony Line."

Mosienko's dazzling moves and scoring knack helped him post a career-high 70 points (goals plus assists) in 1943–44. Max Bentley led the NHL in scoring in both 1945–46 and 1946–47, and he won the 1946 Hart Trophy as the league's Most Valuable Player (MVP). Bentley was among the game's smallest players (5-foot-8 [173 cm] and 158 pounds [72 kg]), but he made up for it with exceptional stick handling and a swift shot.

The Hawks slowly began climbing out of the cellar during the 1953–54 season, although their 12–51–7 record certainly didn't show it. That was the year that former Detroit Red Wings owners John D. Norris and Arthur Wirtz took ownership of the Blackhawks. The team finished in last place, but a large and rangy netminder named Al Rollins gave the new owners at least one thing to smile about, winning the Hart Trophy.

In 1954, Norris and Wirtz hired Tommy Ivan as the team's new general manager. Ivan—who had led the Red Wings to three Stanley Cups—moved

Bill Mosienko WING

Twenty-one seconds. That's all it took Bill Mosienko to score three goals in one incredible game between Chicago and the New York Rangers on March 23, 1952—an NHL record that still stands. Not only did he beat the individual record for fastest hat trick, or three goals in one game (which had been 64 seconds, set by Detroit Red Wings star Carl Liscombe in 1938), he broke the *team* record for the quickest three goals, which had been 24 seconds, set by the Montreal Maroons in 1932. Mosienko played his entire 14-year NHL career with the Blackhawks and was one of just a handful of players of his era to score more than 250 goals.

BLACKHAWKS SEASONS: 1941–55
HEIGHT: 5-8 (173 cm)
WEIGHT: 160 (72.5 kg)

• 1945 Lady Byng Trophy winner (as best sportsman)
• 5-time All-Star
• Career-high 32 goals in 1943–44
• Hockey Hall of Fame inductee (1965)

Goalie Al Rollins spent time with 10 different pro clubs before arriving in Chicago, where in 1954 he won his greatest honor, the Hart Trophy.

quickly to bring in top talent, including wing Ed Litzenberger from the Montreal Canadiens. Litzenberger had an immediate impact in a Hawks sweater, winning the 1955 Calder Trophy.

The Blackhawks' player development system also got an overhaul under the new ownership. The franchise began using a larger network of junior teams and minor-league clubs to groom top talent. Eventually, the expanded system would help the team produce such Hall-of-Famers as wing Bobby Hull, center Stan Mikita, and defenseman Pierre Pilote.

"You know, the funny thing is, everybody thinks we're magicians or something, when all we really do is make the obvious plays..... Each of us knows where the other guys will be."

CHICAGO CENTER STAN MIKITA

Unfortunately, Rollins and Ivan frequently quarreled, and the goalie left town in 1957. To fill the void, the Blackhawks struck a trade with the Red Wings for wing Ted Lindsay and goalie Glenn Hall. Lindsay was a vicious checker who earned the nickname "Terrible Ted." Hall, meanwhile, relished his new opportunity and soon proved himself an NHL star. "So many players are hesitant to go to a team that isn't doing well," said Hall, who would remain in Chicago until 1967. "But we got a chance to lead a team out of the wilderness."

Chicago Versus Canada

BLACKHAWKS OWNER MAJOR McLAUGHLIN was a staunchly patriotic man. He disliked the fact that Canadian teams dominated Stanley Cup play in the NHL's early years, so in the mid-1930s, he set out to fill his roster with American players. When the Blackhawks finished third in the American Division in the 1937–38 season, their first playoff opponents were the mighty Montreal Canadiens. The Blackhawks lost the first game in Montreal, but when the series moved to Chicago, goalie Mike Karakas shut out the Canadiens 4–0 to give the underdog Blackhawks hope. Back in Montreal, the Blackhawks won Game 3 on an overtime goal by wing Mush March.

After beating the New York Americans in the next round of the playoffs, the Blackhawks advanced to the Stanley Cup Finals, where they faced Canada's other powerhouse, the Toronto Maple Leafs. Hopes in Chicago sagged when an injury to Karakas forced the team to call on unknown minor-leaguer Alfie Moore. But Moore allowed just one goal in a Game 1 Blackhawks win, and Karakas returned for Game 3 and helped Chicago topple Toronto three games to one. McLaughlin's team was far from All-American (only about 50 percent), but the Hawks' 1938 championship went down as one of the biggest upsets in Stanley Cup history.

A DYNASTY THAT DISAPPOINTED

SWIFT AND VERSATILE WING BOBBY HULL joined Chicago in 1957, and the star-studded Blackhawks appeared on the verge of dominance as the 1960s began. The 1960–61 Blackhawks started the decade with a bang, setting two club records with 29 wins and 75 points (two points for every win and one point for every tie). In the playoffs, the Hawks upset the defending Stanley Cup champion Canadiens before defeating the Red Wings in six games to capture the Cup. "One of the highlights for me was winning the Stanley Cup that year," goalie Glenn Hall would later say. "I don't think we were supposed to win it then."

Said to deliver the hardest slap shot in hockey (around 120 miles [193 km] per hour), the great Bobby Hull led Chicago back to Stanley Cup glory in 1961.

That Stanley Cup-winning season was the first of 14 consecutive sold-out

seasons at Chicago Stadium. With the Bears football team and the Cubs and

White Sox baseball clubs struggling, the Blackhawks were the biggest game in

town. And Hull, who in 1961–62 became the first Blackhawks player to score

50 goals in a season, was becoming Chicago's favorite athlete.

Another Hawks star of that era was fiesty forward Stan Mikita. In 1963–64,

Mikita ranked near the top of the NHL in penalty minutes, mostly for fight-

ing. Coach Rudy Pilous then took Mikita aside and urged greater self-restraint.

When Mikita took the talk to heart, his career took off. He would win the Art

Ross Trophy four times, and he would bring home the Hart Trophy as league

MVP in 1967 and 1968.

The Hawks added more talent throughout the 1960s, including center Phil

Esposito in 1963. In his first three full seasons with Chicago, Esposito scored

Chris Chelios DEFENSEMAN

In his eight years with the Blackhawks, Chris Chelios earned a reputation as one of the meanest and toughest players in the game. But what really made him special was his offensive prowess. While he was an elite defender, Chelios was also a formidable scorer and gifted passer, and he led Chicago in scoring during the 1995–96 season. Chicago fans loved it when Chelios put a hard check on an opponent and roared any time he dropped his gloves for a fight. He often took opposing forwards out of plays before they even had a chance to shoot.

BLACKHAWKS SEASONS: 1990–99
HEIGHT: 6-1 (180 cm)
WEIGHT: 190 (86 kg)

• 11-time All-Star
• 3-time Norris Trophy winner (as best defenseman)
• 760 career assists
• Chicago defenseman-record 58 assists in 1995–96

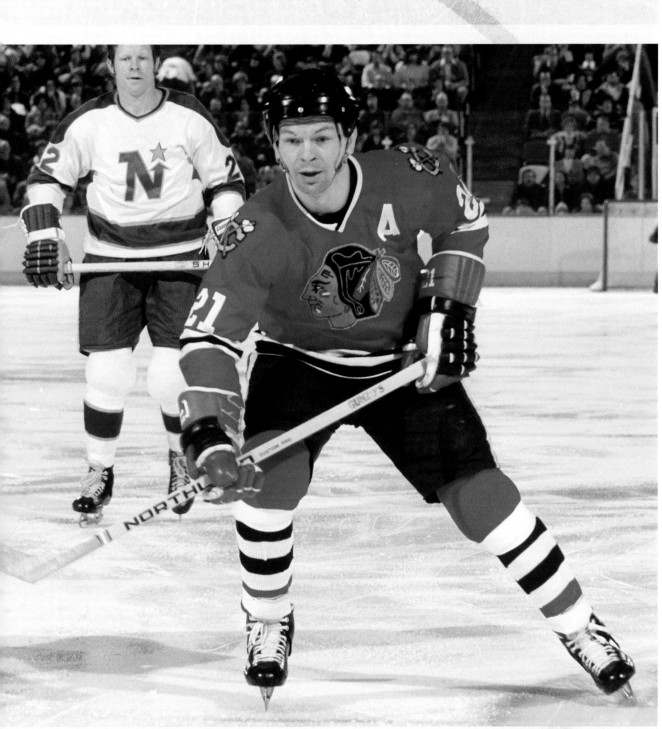

Fan favorite and eight-time All-Star Stan Mikita capped his long career with induction into the Hall of Fame, going in in 1983 with Bobby Hull.

23, 27, and 21 goals. Also in the mix by the end of the 1964–65 season was winger Ken Hodge, whose 6-foot-2 (183 cm) and 210-pound (95 kg) frame made him a natural "policeman" on the ice. Hodge played the role of enforcer because the rest of the team was relatively small, but it limited his offensive contributions and didn't square with his personality. "I wound up in my fair share of fights," Hodge later said. "But it's not really my nature. I don't like playing the bully."

In 1964–65, Dennis Hull skated alongside his star brother, Bobby, at wing for the Blackhawks. Dennis established himself as a reliable scorer with a mighty slap shot that rivaled—and some believed surpassed—his older brother's. During his time with the Blackhawks, the younger Hull settled into a talented line that included center Pit Martin and wing Jim Pappin.

In 1966–67, the Blackhawks' 41–17–12 record earned them a first-place regular-season finish in the NHL for the first time in franchise history. After three more winning seasons but fruitless playoff appearances in the late 1960s, the Blackhawks made defense their focus as the '70s began. Goalie Tony Esposito captured the Vezina Trophy in 1970, 1972, and 1974. Esposito's flamboyant "butterfly" style and dramatic flops on the ice for saves ranked him among the league's most successful and entertaining goalies.

"When Bobby [Hull] was on the ice for 30 minutes a game, the other teams had to worry about him all that time. They couldn't get very ambitious themselves because Bobby would burn them at the other end."

CHICAGO GOALIE TONY ESPOSITO

Known for his dramatic, goal-saving flops on the ice, goalie Tony Esposito helped the Blackhawks make the playoffs in each of his 15 Chicago seasons.

In 1972, the Blackhawks suffered a staggering loss when Bobby Hull left Chicago for the World Hockey Association's (WHA) Winnipeg Jets. The Jets offered him a $1-million contract, which made him the world's highest-paid hockey player. The Blackhawks immediately saw their attendance drop, their play suffer, and their chance to become a true dynasty fade. "It's harder to lose someone in life than in death," said Blackhawks president Bill Wirtz. "That was the case with Bobby Hull. He was such an infectious star in this market."

Led by coach Billy Reay and such standouts as Mikita, Martin, and center Ivan Boldirev, the Blackhawks finished first in their division seven times in the 1970s, but they managed to reach the Stanley Cup Finals just twice, losing both times to the Montreal Canadiens (in 1971 and 1973). As the 1980s approached, the Blackhawks began looking for new talent.

"In coaching hockey, the important thing is psychology. You have to know which players to goad and which ones to praise. And you have to know when and how to go about it."

CHICAGO COACH BILLY REAY

Keenan's Punishment

DEFENSEMAN CHRIS CHELIOS BECAME one of the Blackhawks' best players after he was traded from the Montreal Canadiens in 1990. Back in Montreal later that year, Chelios was nervous about facing his old team. So, the night before the game, Chelios and line-mate Steve Smith hit the town to take their minds off the tension and returned to their hotel well after curfew. On their way to the elevator, they passed coach Mike Keenan. The coach said nothing to the pair in spite of the late hour. "Is it possible he didn't see us?" Chelios asked Smith after the elevator doors closed. During warm-ups the next day, Keenan again said nothing about the curfew violation. Both players wondered whether they might be benched but found themselves in the starting lineup. Two minutes into the game, a whistle blew, and Chelios and Smith skated toward the bench for a line change. Keenan pointed them back on the ice. At the next whistle, the pair again returned to the bench, but Keenan again turned them away. Suddenly the players knew that Coach Keenan *had* seen them. The pair skated to near exhaustion for more than 40 minutes without a break in a 4–2 Blackhawks loss.

STARS, BUT
STILL NO CUP

CHICAGO FOUND SOME NEW TALENT IN THE form of a promising center named Denis Savard. Savard was selected third overall in the 1980 NHL Draft and got off to a fast start. In his rookie season, the center scored 28 goals with 47 assists. Despite his average size (5-foot-10 [178 cm] and 175 pounds [79 kg]), "Savvy" was a physical force on the ice. He also employed a trademark move in which he spun his body all the way around the puck, confusing defenders and goalies.

Savard was the middle man in a terrific front line that included Steve Larmer at right wing. Larmer was an unremarkable skater and shooter, but he paired up seamlessly with Al Secord at left wing. "We were so comfortable and so in sync with each other on the ice, we hardly had to discuss anything," Secord said. "If we did make changes, we'd do it with one or two words and that was it."

A fast skater, slick passer, and creative scorer, offensive dynamo Denis Savard thrilled Chicago fans with many highlight-reel plays in the 1980s.

That front trio scored 132 goals during the 1982–83 season, and Larmer earned Rookie of the Year honors. The team rolled to a 47–23–10 record that year, winning the Campbell Conference's Norris Division (the league was split into Campbell and Wales Conferences in 1974) but losing to the Edmonton Oilers in the conference finals. The Blackhawks would make the playoffs every year in the 1980s but never advance to the Cup Finals.

The late '80s ushered in a new era featuring a young center named Jeremy Roenick. Roenick was a physical player and an emotional leader who gave the Blackhawks a jolt of energy with his 1988 arrival. His flashy stick-handling and swift skating would soon make him one of the NHL's top scorers, as he would post more than 100 points each season from 1991–92 to 1993–94.

Also in 1988, the Blackhawks hired a fiery new coach named Mike Keenan. The coach came to the Blackhawks from the Philadelphia Flyers, a team he had

Pierre Pilote DEFENSEMAN

Pierre "Pete" Pilote, one of the most feared defensemen of his era, got his start playing street hockey, and his first pair of skates was his mother's. Although relatively small, Pilote had a big reputation that stemmed mainly from a scuffle he once had with Montreal Canadiens stars Henri and Maurice Richard, in which he got the best of both brothers. Pilote was known for diving and blocking shots without fear—and without a helmet or facemask. In spite of his risky style of play, Pilote once played 376 games in a row before he was sidelined with a dislocated shoulder.

BLACKHAWKS SEASONS: 1955–68
HEIGHT: 5-10 (178 cm)
WEIGHT: 165 (75 kg)

• 8-time All-Star
• 3-time Norris Trophy winner
• 418 career assists
• Hockey Hall of Fame inductee (1975)

Although Jeremy Roenick was an elite scorer, breaking the 50-goal mark in both 1991–92 and 1992–93, he never shied away from physical play.

helped rebuild into a Stanley Cup contender. Keenan brought an intense—some said military-like—leadership style to the Blackhawks, stressing physical conditioning, grueling practices, and perfection during games.

With Keenan behind the bench and veterans such as Larmer, goalie Ed Belfour, and defenseman Chris Chelios alongside Roenick, the Blackhawks battled all the way to the 1992 Stanley Cup Finals. The excitement ended abruptly, though, as Chicago lost to the Pittsburgh Penguins in four straight games.

"The fans were unbelievable. The noise was deafening. There was nothing like it in the league!"

CHICAGO WING AL SECORD,
ON PLAYING IN CHICAGO STADIUM

The early 1990s saw the Blackhawks move into a new arena and continue their winning ways. They left beloved and boisterous Chicago Stadium for the new United Center, located across Madison Street, in 1994. But by 1996–97, the Hawks were once again a struggling club, and by 1997–98, Chelios was the only player that remained from their All-Star lineup earlier in the decade. The 1997–98 season ended with a 30–39–13 mark, and Chicago missed the playoffs for the first time in 29 years.

A Rain of Hats

IN GAME 4 OF THE 1992 STANLEY CUP FINALS, the Blackhawks faced a do-or-die situation. They were down three games to zero against the Pittsburgh Penguins and needing a victory at Chicago Stadium to stay alive in the best-of-seven series. Wing and team captain Dirk Graham did his best to keep Chicago in contention. Early in the first period, Graham took a pass from defenseman Chris Chelios and scored his first goal. Just 30 seconds later, Graham again took a feed from Chelios and netted another goal. The captain pulled off the hat trick when he scored his third goal of the game with almost four minutes left in the period. The Chicago fans went wild and began removing their hats and tossing them onto the rink. When the flurry of headwear-throwing ended, 311 hats littered the ice. At the end of the first period, the score was tied 3–3, thanks to Graham's solo effort. His heroics would not be enough to stave off elimination (the Blackhawks lost the game 6–5), but they earned Graham a special place in the team record books—and an assortment of hats that were later donated to charity.

THE HAWKS SOAR ON

THE BLACKHAWKS LIMPED INTO THE NEW century, missing the playoffs again in 2000. In 2001–02, they finally returned to form, finishing 41–27–13 and skating back to the playoffs. But the Hawks lost to the St. Louis Blues in the first round.

Chicago slipped below .500 in 2002–03, finishing third among the five teams in the Western Conference's Central Division (the league was divided into Eastern and Western Conferences in 1993). Wing Steve Sullivan led the team offensively with 26 goals and 35 assists. Many Chicago fans were disappointed when Sullivan—a fan favorite due to his scoring skills on the ice and engaging personality off of it—was traded to the Nashville Predators the following season. In 2003–04, quick center Tyler Arnason emerged as Chicago's top offensive threat.

Steve Sullivan started his NHL career slowly in New Jersey and Toronto before arriving in Chicago in 1999 and developing into a standout.

A dispute between NHL players and owners over salaries resulted in the cancellation of the 2004–05 season. In 2005, with the conflict finally resolved, Chicago's new general manager, Dale Tallon, began building the team back into a contender.

Denis Savard took over as head coach in 2006, putting one of the all-time Chicago greats in charge of his favorite team. The Hall of Fame center became the 36th head coach of the Blackhawks, but his on-ice experience didn't translate into immediate success. The Blackhawks finished the 2006–07 season with a record of 31–42–9, in 11th place in the Western Conference and out of the playoffs for the eighth time in nine years.

In 2007, winger Martin Havlat gave fans in the Windy City something to cheer about when he scored two goals in the NHL All-Star Game to help lift his Western Conference squad to a 12–9 victory over the Eastern All-Stars.

Glenn Hall GOALIE

Glenn Hall is widely regarded as one of the greatest NHL goalies of all time. He is even credited with inventing the now-popular "butterfly" method of goaltending, in which goalies drop to their knees and spread their feet to the sides to block low shots—a pioneering style that helped him earn the nickname "Mr. Goalie." But Hall may be better known for a record that will never be broken. From 1955 to 1963, he played 502 games in a row without a facemask or helmet. His streak ended on November 8, 1963, when a back injury forced him out of the lineup.

BLACKHAWKS SEASONS: 1957–67
HEIGHT: 5-11 (180 cm)
WEIGHT: 190 (86 kg)

- 13-time All-Star
- 3-time Vezina Trophy winner (as best goaltender)
- 1956 Calder Trophy winner (as Rookie of the Year)
- Hockey Hall of Fame inductee (1975)

Nicknamed "Mach 9" due to his great speed, Martin Havlat netted 25 goals and a place on the All-Star team in 2006–07, his first season in Chicago.

Havlat, who had arrived in a 2006 trade with the Ottawa Senators, was one of several talented young teammates who gave the Blackhawks faithful some hope for future success.

Skating alongside Havlat was fellow wing Radim Vrbata, who notched 27 assists in 2006–07. In May 2007, the Blackhawks added more depth by signing Jonathan Toews, a promising young center selected with the third overall pick in the 2006 NHL Draft, to a three-year deal. In 2007–08, Toews took the ice alongside rookie sensation Patrick Kane, a wing who was chosen with the first overall pick in the 2007 NHL Draft. "They're special," Coach Savard said of the two young stars. "They want to be the best, not only once in a while, but every night."

"I'd like to have a reputation as a good person, the kind who is good to people and they're good back to you. Off the ice, that is."

CHICAGO DEFENSEMAN CHRIS CHELIOS

By 2007, it had been four long decades since the Blackhawks last hoisted the Stanley Cup. But with a history of surprising seasons such as the 1938 miracle, a roster of all-time greats such as Bobby Hull, and the backing of a city full of passionate and vocal fans, the Blackhawks might very well be hosting another Cup celebration soon.

42

From Buds to Hawks

WHEN THE WESTERN HOCKEY LEAGUE (WHL) was going out of business in 1926, Major Frederic McLaughlin saw an opportunity to bring hockey to Chicago. He bought the WHL's Portland Rosebuds franchise for $200,000 before the start of the 1926–27 NHL season but decided the squad needed a new name. As a former commander of the 333rd Machine Gun Battalion for the U.S. Army during World War I, McLaughlin had belonged to the 86th Division—a group of soldiers who called themselves "Black Hawks." He felt the name "Blackhawks" captured a piece of his own history and also paid tribute to an American Indian leader named Chief Black Hawk, who had roamed the midwestern plains as head of the Sauk tribe. McLaughlin's wife, Irene Castle—a famous ballroom dancer—designed the team's distinct black-and-white striped uniforms featuring the head of Chief Black Hawk, completing the Rosebuds' transformation. In 1955, longtime Chicago coach Tommy Ivan's wife tweaked the uniform's design, dropping the horizontal stripes from the chest and adding crossed tomahawks on the shoulders. And although the name Blackhawks was originally spelled as two words, it was presented as either one word or two for most of the team's history. The one-word name was finally made official in 1985.

Although Chicago missed the playoffs for the fourth straight year in 2006–07, rising players such as Radim Vrbata promised to end the drought.

Billy Reay COACH

Billy Reay was an accomplished center before he became the Blackhawks' most successful coach. Reay, who took the Hawks to three Stanley Cup Finals between 1965 and 1973, was known as much for his style of dress as his coaching skill. He always wore a sharp-looking suit and a red fedora with a Blackhawks logo when he stood behind the bench. By the time he retired in 1976, Reay had accumulated 599 coaching victories, making him one of the winningest coaches in hockey history. Even after his retirement, Reay remained a regular presence at Blackhawks games and practices.

BLACKHAWKS SEASONS AS COACH: 1963–77
NHL COACHING RECORD: 599–445–175
STANLEY CUP APPEARANCES WITH CHICAGO: 1965, 1971, 1973

INDEX